PRAISE FOR THE *MARCH* TRILOGY

March: Book One
128 pages, $14.95 (US)
ISBN: 978-1-60309-300-2

March: Book Two
192 pages, $19.95 (US)
ISBN: 978-1-60309-400-9

March: Book Three
256 pages, $19.99 (US)
ISBN: 978-1-60309-402-3

March (Trilogy Slipcase Set)
Three Volumes, $49.99 (US)
ISBN: 978-1-60309-395-8

**#1 *New York Times* and *Washington Post* Bestseller
National Book Award
Will Eisner Comic Industry Award
Coretta Scott King Book Award—Author Honor
Robert F. Kennedy Book Award—Special Recognition
Street Literature Book Award Medal
ALA Notable Books
YALSA's Top 10 Great Graphic Novels for Teens
YALSA's Outstanding Books for the College Bound
Reader's Digest's Graphic Novels Every Grown-Up Should Read
Added to New York City Schools curriculum and taught in over 40 states
Selected for college & university reading programs across America**

"Congressman John Lewis has been a resounding moral voice in the quest for equality for more than 50 years, and I'm so pleased that he is sharing his memories of the Civil Rights Movement with America's young leaders. In *March*, he brings a whole new generation with him across the Edmund Pettus Bridge, from a past of clenched fists into a future of outstretched hands."
—President Bill Clinton

"With *March*, Congressman John Lewis takes us behind the scenes of some of the most pivotal moments of the Civil Rights Movement. In graphic novel form, his first-hand account makes these historic events both accessible and relevant to an entire new generation of Americans."
— LeVar Burton

"*March* is one of the most important graphic novels ever created—an extraordinary presentation of an extraordinary life, and proof that young people can change the world. I'm stunned by the power of these comics, and grateful that Congressman Lewis's story will enlighten and inspire future generations of readers and leaders."
— Raina Telgemeier

"There is perhaps no more important modern book to be stocked in American school libraries than *March*."
— *The Washington Post*

"Essential reading...*March* is a moving and important achievement...the story of a true American superhero."
—*USA Today*

"Emphasizing disruption, decentralization and cooperation over the mythic ascent of heroic leaders, this graphic novel's presentation of civil rights is startlingly contemporary."
— *The New York Times*

"Superbly told history."
—*Publishers Weekly* (starred review)

"Powell captures the danger and tension in stunning cinematic spreads, which dramatically complement Lewis's powerful story…The story of the civil rights movement is a triumphant one, but Lewis's account is full of nuance and personal struggle, both of which impart an empowering human element to an often mythologized period of history…this is a must-read."
— *Booklist* (starred review)

"An astonishingly accomplished graphic memoir that brings to life a vivid portrait of the civil rights era, Lewis's extraordinary history and accomplishments, and the movement he helped lead…Its power, accessibility and artistry destine it for awards, and a well-deserved place at the pinnacle of the comics canon."
—NPR

"*March* provides a potent reminder that the sit-ins, far from being casually assembled, were well-coordinated, disciplined events informed by a rigorous philosophy…Likely to prove inspirational to readers for years to come."
—*Barnes and Noble Review*

"A riveting chronicle of Lewis's extraordinary life…it powerfully illustrates how much perseverance is needed to achieve fundamental social change."
—*O, The Oprah Magazine*

"*March* offers a poignant portrait of an iconic figure that both entertains and edifies, and deserves to be placed alongside other historical graphic memoirs like *Persepolis* and *Maus*."
—*Entertainment Weekly*

"The civil rights movement can seem to some like a distant memory…John Lewis refreshes our memories in dramatic fashion."
—*The Chicago Tribune*

"When a graphic novel tries to interest young readers in an important topic, it often feels forced. Not so with the exhilarating *March*…Powerful words and pictures."
—*The Boston Globe*

"This memoir puts a human face on a struggle that many students will primarily know from textbooks… Visually stunning, the black-and-white illustrations convey the emotions of this turbulent time…This insider's view of the civil rights movement should be required reading for young and old; not to be missed."
—*School Library Journal* (starred review)

"A powerful tale of courage and principle igniting sweeping social change, told by a strong-minded, uniquely qualified eyewitness…The heroism of those who sat and marched…comes through with vivid, inspiring clarity."
—*Kirkus Reviews* (starred review)

"Lewis's remarkable life has been skillfully translated into graphics…Segregation's insult to personhood comes across here with a visual, visceral punch. This version of Lewis's life story belongs in libraries to teach readers about the heroes of America."
—*Library Journal* (starred review)

"Powell's drawings in *March* combine the epic sweep of history with the intimate personal details of memoir, and bring Lewis's story to life in a way that feels entirely unfamiliar. *March* is shaping up to be a major work of history and graphic literature."
—*Slate*

"In a new graphic memoir, the civil rights leader shows youth how to get in trouble—good trouble."
—*In These Times*

To the past and future children
of the movement.

THIS IS AN UNLAWFUL ASSEMBLY!

YOUR MARCH IS NOT CONDUCIVE TO THE PUBLIC SAFETY-- YOU ARE ORDERED TO **DISPERSE** AND GO BACK TO YOUR CHURCH OR TO YOUR HOMES!

MAY WE HAVE A WORD WITH THE MAJOR?

MAY WE HAVE A WORD WITH

THERE IS NO WORD TO BE HAD.

YOU HAVE TWO MINUTES TO TURN AROUND AND GO BACK TO YOUR CHURCH.

THERE IS NO WORD TO BE HAD.

we should kneel and pray, Hosea.

'S BRIDGE

TROOPERS--

ADVANCE!

BOOK ONE

JOHN LEWIS

ANDREW AYDIN

NATE POWELL

WASHINGTON, D.C.
JANUARY 20, 2009.

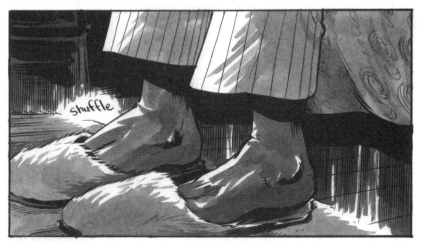

♪ but you cannot take my ♪ dignity...

CANNON HOUSE
OFFICE BUILDING

KLIK

SQUEE
SQUEE

...and no one could find him till that school bus would come whirring down that dirt road.

--FROM SOME PLACE OR ANOTHER, UNDER THE PORCH MOST TIMES, HE WOU-- BOB*!

HELLO, ROSA! HOW ARE YOU?

* MY CHILDHOOD NICKNAME.

BABY BROTHER, YOU LOOK COLD. WHERE'S YOUR HAT, YOUR SCARF?

I'M FINE-- I'LL BE OKAY.

YOU TWO HAVE YOUR TICKETS? ANDREW WILL TAKE YOU IN A FEW MINUTES TO--

KNOCK KNOCK

COME IN.

HI--

ARE YOU OPEN?

WE'RE FROM ATLANTA, AND WE'VE COME FOR THE INAUGURATION-- I WAS BRINGING MY BOYS HERE SO THEY COULD SEE JOHN LEWIS' OFFICE.

OF COURSE, OF COURSE-- COME ON IN.

CAN I GET YOU SOMETHING TO DRINK?

COKE, MAYBE SOME WATER?

YOU--

YOU-- YOU'RE JOHN LEWIS!

YES.

UH, WELL--

UMMM I'M SORRY TO DISTURB YOU, I JUST, I MEAN WE JUST--

CONGRESSMAN LEWIS, THESE ARE MY TWO SONS, JACOB and ESAU.

HELLO, IT'S VERY NICE TO MEET YOU. I'M JOHN LEWIS.

WOULD YOU LIKE TO SEE MY OFFICE?

CONGRESSMAN LEWIS, I CAN'T BELIEVE YOU'RE HERE.

WE STOPPED BY BECAUSE I WANTED MY BOYS TO SEE THEIR HISTORY-- I WANTED THEM TO KNOW--

AS A CHILD, MY PARENTS GAVE ME THE RESPONSIBILITY OF TAKING CARE OF OUR FAMILY'S CHICKENS.

WE LIVED ON 110 ACRES OF
COTTON, CORN, AND PEANUT FIELDS
IN A LITTLE CORNER OF
PIKE COUNTY, ALABAMA.

MY FATHER BOUGHT IT IN
THE SPRING OF 1940 FOR $300.

CASH.

IT WAS EVERY PENNY MY FATHER HAD TO HIS NAME, MONEY EARNED BY TENANT FARMING.

THUD

MY FATHER WAS A SHARECROPPER.

I NEVER HAD ANY FEELINGS ABOUT THE OTHER ANIMALS ON OUR FARM,

CREAK

BUT I WAS ALWAYS DRAWN TO THE CHICKENS.

I NEVER TOOK THE CHICKENS STRAIGHT TO THE YARD TO FEED THEM--

bok

I FELT THE NEED TO TALK TO THEM FIRST.

chick-chick-chick-CHICKIES!
chick-chick-chick-CHICKIES! ♫

NO ONE ELSE COULD TELL THOSE CHICKENS APART, AND NO ONE CARED TO.

THERE WERE RHODE ISLAND REDS,

DOMINIQUES,

and BANTAMS.

I KNEW EVERY ONE OF THEM BY APPEARANCE AND PERSONALITY. THEY WERE EACH INDIVIDUALS TO ME.

SOME I EVEN NAMED.

BIG BELLE, FOR INSTANCE-- SHE FELL DOWN THE WELL.

IT TOOK US FIVE DAYS TO GET HER OUT.

WE FINALLY PUT SOME BREAD CRUMBS IN A BASKET AND LOWERED IT DOWN.

DARNED IF SHE DIDN'T CLIMB RIGHT IN THAT BASKET.

THEN THERE WAS LI'L PULLET, MY FAVORITE. SHE LIVED LONGER THAN ANY OTHER BIRD I HAD.

EVERYWHERE I WENT AROUND THE CHICKEN YARD, LI'L PULLET WOULD BE RIGHT THERE BEHIND ME.

SPRINGTIME WAS MY FAVORITE TIME OF YEAR BECAUSE IT WAS THE ONLY SEASON WE COULD GET BABY CHICKS.

WHEN THE HENS BEGAN LAYING THEIR EGGS, I'D MARK EACH ONE WITH A LIGHTLY PENCILED NUMBER TO HELP KEEP TRACK OF ITS PROGRESS DURING THE THREE WEEKS IT TOOK TO HATCH.

THE NUMBERS WERE ALWAYS ODD. NEVER EVEN. I HAD BEEN TOLD NEVER TO PUT AN EVEN NUMBER UNDER A SETTING HEN.

IT WAS BAD LUCK.

AND I WOULD CHEAT ON THOSE SETTING HENS.

I'D TAKE A FEW FROM THE HENS THAT WERE SETTING ON A LARGE NUMBER OF EGGS, AND SLIP THEM UNDER THE HENS THAT WEREN'T.

THIS CUT DOWN ON THE NUMBER OF "BAD" EGGS.

I ALSO LEARNED THAT A HEN WILL CONTINUE TO SET AS LONG AS SHE HAS EGGS UNDERNEATH HER.

SO BY SLIPPING MORE EGGS UNDER MY HENS, I WAS ABLE TO KEEP THEM SETTING ANOTHER THREE WEEKS.

STRETCHING OUT THAT PROCESS IS NOT NATURAL, AND IT TOOK A TOLL.

SO, I BUILT A MAKESHIFT INCUBATOR.

IT WORKED.

I ALWAYS HOPED TO SAVE ENOUGH MONEY FOR AN ACTUAL INCUBATOR, LIKE THE $18.95 MODEL ADVERTISED IN THE SEARS-ROEBUCK CATALOG.

WE CALLED THAT CATALOG OUR WISH BOOK.

BY THE TIME I WAS FIVE I COULD READ IT MYSELF, AND ONE PHRASE STRUCK ME STRONGLY, THOUGH I COULDN'T COMPREHEND ITS FULL MEANING AT THE TIME--

BEHOLD THE LAMB OF GOD WHICH TAKETH AWAY THE SIN OF THE WORLD.

SO I PREACHED TO MY CHICKENS JUST ABOUT EVERY NIGHT.

ahem.

b. kaw!

I WOULD GET THEM ALL INTO THE HENHOUSE AND SETTLE THEM ON THEIR ROOSTS.

THEY WOULD SIT QUIETLY.

Blessed are the meek: for they shall inherit the earth.

Blessed are they which do hunger and thirst after righteousness: for they shall be filled.

Blessed are the pure in heart: for they shall see God.

THEY WOULD BOW THEIR HEADS,

BUT THEY WOULD NEVER QUITE SAY AMEN.

THEY WOULD SHAKE THEIR HEADS,

Blessed are the merciful: for they shall obtain mercy.

Blessed are the peacemakers: for they shall be called the children of God.

I IMAGINED THAT THEY WERE MY CONGREGATION,

AND ME--

Blessed are they which are persecuted for righteousness' sake:

for theirs is the kingdom of heaven.

I WAS A PREACHER.

OF COURSE, ANYONE CAN FIGURE OUT THE DANGER OF MAKING PETS OUT OF FARM ANIMALS--

ESPECIALLY CHICKENS.

YOU GET EMOTIONALLY ATTACHED TO AN ANIMAL DESTINED FOR THE DINNER TABLE, AND YOU'RE ASKING FOR A BROKEN HEART.

BUT I COULDN'T HELP IT.

MORE OFTEN THAN I LIKED, A GROWN HEN OR EVEN A CHICK WOULD DIE OF MORE NATURAL CAUSES.

FOR THESE BIRDS, I WOULD CONDUCT A FUNERAL.

THIS WAS **NOT** CHILD'S PLAY. I WAS GENUINELY GRIEF-STRICKEN, AND THE SERVICES WERE PAINSTAKINGLY PRECISE.

I WOULD GATHER WHICHEVER OF MY SISTERS AND BROTHERS AND COUSINS I COULD.

AND I WOULD DELIVER A EULOGY.

MY PARENTS WOULD WATCH THE NEWEST TINY COFFIN JOIN THE NEAT ROW OF SMALL DIRT-MOUNDED GRAVES,

AND WONDER WHAT KIND OF SON THEY HAD.

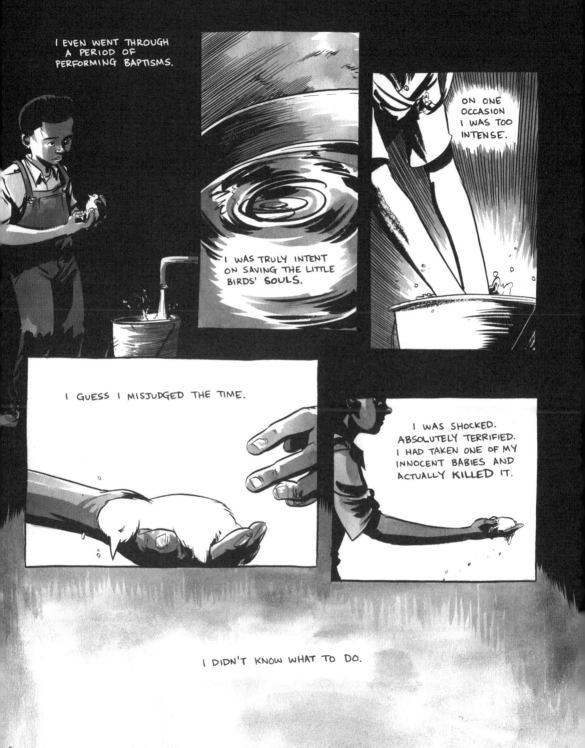

I EVEN WENT THROUGH A PERIOD OF PERFORMING BAPTISMS.

I WAS TRULY INTENT ON SAVING THE LITTLE BIRDS' SOULS.

ON ONE OCCASION I WAS TOO INTENSE.

I GUESS I MISJUDGED THE TIME.

I WAS SHOCKED. ABSOLUTELY TERRIFIED. I HAD TAKEN ONE OF MY INNOCENT BABIES AND ACTUALLY KILLED IT.

I DIDN'T KNOW WHAT TO DO.

ALL THESE ASPECTS OF MY CHICKEN PLAY TICKLED
MY PARENTS AT FIRST, BUT THEIR AMUSEMENT VANISHED
AS I BEGAN SERIOUSLY PROTESTING THEIR OWN
TREATMENT OF THE BIRDS.

FROM TIME TO TIME, THEY WOULD HAVE NO CASH
TO PAY THE ROLLING STORE MAN FOR SOME SORELY-NEEDED
SUGAR OR FLOUR, SO THEY WOULD OFFER
A BIRD IN BARTER INSTEAD.

ONE OF **MY** CHICKENS.

I'D CRY, REFUSE TO SPEAK TO THEM FOR THE REST OF THE DAY-- EVEN SKIP THAT EVENING'S MEAL.

WORSE, THOUGH, WAS WATCHING MY MOTHER OR FATHER KILL ONE OF THE CHICKENS FOR A SPECIAL SUNDAY DINNER.

THEY WOULD EITHER BREAK ITS NECK WITH THEIR HANDS,

SPINNING IT AROUND UNTIL THE BONE S N A P P E D

OR SIMPLY CHOP THE HEAD OFF.

I WAS NOWHERE TO BE SEEN AT THOSE FAMILY MEALS.

THEY WOULD THEN DRAIN THE BLOOD FROM ITS BODY AND DIP IT IN BOILING WATER, SCALDING IT TO LOOSEN ITS FEATHERS FOR PLUCKING.

so you stopped raising chickens because it was too hard to see them be killed?

NO--

THE DEATH OF THOSE CHICKENS WAS JUST A PART OF LIFE.

BUT EVENTUALLY, I BEGAN SPENDING MORE TIME DOING SCHOOLWORK, STUDYING, AND MY EYES BEGAN OPENING TO THE WORLD AROUND ME.

but--

why did you need to study more?

did you fail your tests?

JACOB! shhhh!

I DID OKAY. I WASN'T THE BEST.

what?!

BUT SCHOOL WAS IMPORTANT TO ME, AND IT WAS ULTIMATELY THE REASON I GOT INVOLVED IN THE CIVIL RIGHTS MOVEMENT.

THE THING IS, WHEN I WAS YOUNG, THERE **WASN'T** MUCH OF A CIVIL RIGHTS MOVEMENT. I WANTED TO WORK AT **SOMETHING**, BUT GROWING UP IN RURAL ALABAMA, MY PARENTS KNEW IT COULD BE **DANGEROUS** TO MAKE ANY WAVES.

stay out of trouble.

don't get in white people's way.

BUT OTHER MEMBERS OF MY FAMILY HELPED OPEN MY EYES.

IN THE SUMMER OF 1951, I TOOK MY FIRST TRIP NORTH.

OTIS CARTER, ONE OF MY MOTHER'S BROTHERS, ARRANGED THE JOURNEY. HE PLANNED IT COMPLETELY FOR MY SAKE.

HE LIVED IN DOTHAN, ABOUT SIXTY MILES SOUTH OF US, WHERE HE WAS A TEACHER AND A SCHOOL PRINCIPAL.

I WAS SO SERIOUS, VERY EARNEST, STILL SERMONIZING WITH MY CHICKENS, STILL PROTESTING WHEN THAT WHITE MEAT WENT ON THE TABLE.

UNCLE OTIS HAD ALWAYS TAKEN A SPECIAL INTEREST IN ME, ESPECIALLY AS I BEGAN TO GROW AND STAND OUT A LITTLE BIT--

NOT JUST WITH MY DEVOTION TO SCHOOLWORK, BUT WITH THE WAY I GENERALLY ACTED.

I WORE A TIE OFTEN, AND SOME OF THE GROWNUPS TEASED ME ABOUT THAT, TELLING ME I DRESSED LIKE A PREACHER.

I KNOW NOW THAT UNCLE OTIS SAW SOMETHING IN ME THAT I HADN'T YET SEEN.

THAT IS WHY WE TOOK OUR TRIP IN JUNE OF '51.

THERE WOULD BE NO RESTAURANTS FOR US TO STOP AT UNTIL WE WERE **WELL** OUT OF THE SOUTH,

SO WE CARRIED OUR RESTAURANT RIGHT IN THE CAR WITH US.

STOPPING FOR GAS AND BATHROOM BREAKS TOOK CAREFUL PLANNING. UNCLE OTIS HAD MADE THIS TRIP BEFORE, AND HE KNEW WHICH PLACES ALONG THE WAY OFFERED "COLORED" BATHROOMS--

AND WHICH WERE SAFER TO JUST PASS ON BY.

ALABAMA.

TENNESSEE.

KENTUCKY.

THESE WERE THE STATES WE
HAD TO BE CAREFUL IN AS WE
MADE OUR WAY NORTH.

you are now leaving
Alabama
and entering
Tennessee
"TENNESSEE — AMERICA AT ITS BEST"

IT WASN'T UNTIL WE GOT INTO OHIO

THAT I COULD FEEL UNCLE OTIS RELAX--

you are now entering OHIO
THE BUCKEYE STATE WELCOMES YOU

AND SO I RELAXED, TOO.

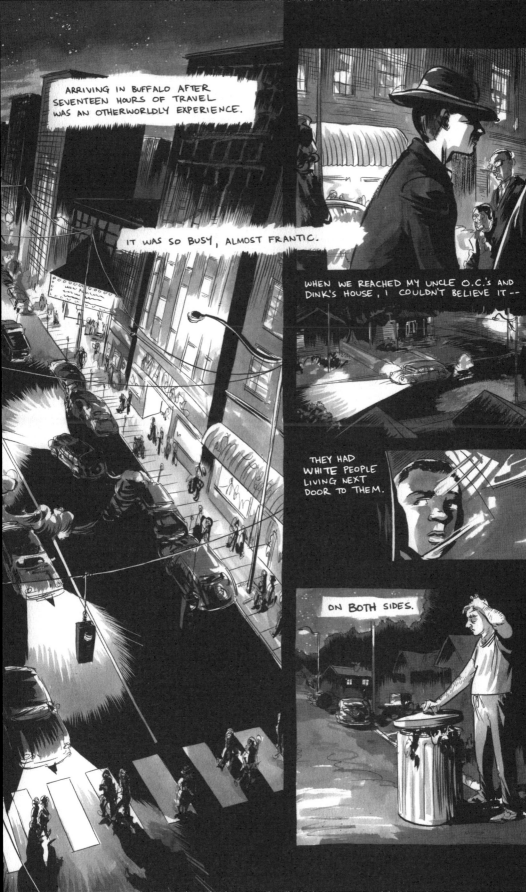

ARRIVING IN BUFFALO AFTER SEVENTEEN HOURS OF TRAVEL WAS AN OTHERWORLDLY EXPERIENCE.

IT WAS SO BUSY, ALMOST FRANTIC.

WHEN WE REACHED MY UNCLE O.C.'s AND DINK'S HOUSE, I COULDN'T BELIEVE IT--

THEY HAD WHITE PEOPLE LIVING NEXT DOOR TO THEM.

ON BOTH SIDES.

MY AUNT LEOLA AND AUNT MAE CHARLES TOOK ME SHOPPING DOWNTOWN ONE DAY AT A DEPARTMENT STORE CALLED SATTLER'S.

THERE, FOR THE FIRST TIME IN MY LIFE, I RODE AN ESCALATOR.

I HAD NEVER EVEN **HEARD** OF SUCH A THING.

I FOUND MY WAY TO THE CANDY COUNTER AND IT WAS LIKE **MAGIC**.

I TRIED TO MAKE THAT BAG OF NEAPOLITAN CANDY LAST FOREVER.

ANOTHER TIME, WE WENT TO THE OUTDOOR MARKET AND I WATCHED MY AUNT LEOLA SHOP FOR A CHICKEN.

CITY PEOPLE DIDN'T RAISE THEIR OWN CHICKENS. THEY DID WHAT MY AUNT DID--

I WANT THAT ONE.

THAT AMAZED ME. IT WAS SO DIFFERENT FROM BACK HOME.

I WASN'T EVEN BOTHERED BY THE FATE OF THESE CHICKENS.

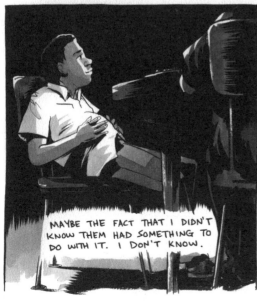

MAYBE THE FACT THAT I DIDN'T KNOW THEM HAD SOMETHING TO DO WITH IT. I DON'T KNOW.

I DO KNOW THAT I HAD NO PROBLEM CLEANING MY PLATE THAT EVENING.

BY LATE AUGUST WHEN IT WAS
TIME TO RETURN TO ALABAMA,
I WAS MORE THAN READY.

I MISSED MY BROTHERS AND SISTERS.

I MISSED MY PARENTS.

WHEN I FINALLY ARRIVED HOME,
I WAS CRYING BECAUSE IT
FELT SO GOOD TO BE BACK.

thank you,
uncle otis.

AFTER THAT TRIP,
HOME NEVER FELT THE SAME,
AND NEITHER DID I.

IN THE FALL, I STARTED RIDING
THE BUS TO SCHOOL, WHICH
SHOULD'VE BEEN FUN.

BUT IT WAS JUST ANOTHER
SAD REMINDER OF HOW DIFFERENT
OUR LIVES WERE FROM THOSE
OF WHITE CHILDREN.

LEWIS

THE COUNTY DIDN'T BOTHER PAVING ROADS INTO "COLORED" COMMUNITIES UNLESS IT WAS NECESSARY FOR WHITE TRAFFIC TO PASS THROUGH.

OUR BUS ITSELF WAS AN OLD HAND-ME-DOWN, JUST LIKE OUR SCHOOLBOOKS.

I REALIZED HOW OLD IT WAS WHEN WE FINALLY CLIMBED ONTO THE PAVED HIGHWAY, THE MAIN ROAD RUNNING EAST FROM TROY, AND PASSED THE WHITE CHILDREN'S BUSES.

WE PASSED THEIR SCHOOLHOUSES AS WELL, WITH NICE PLAYGROUND EQUIPMENT OUTSIDE -- NOTHING LIKE OUR CLUSTER OF SMALL CINDERBLOCK BUILDINGS WITH A DIRT FIELD OUT BACK FOR RECESS.

WE DROVE PAST PRISON WORK GANGS ALMOST EVERY DAY. THE PRISONERS WERE ALWAYS BLACK.

AS WERE THE FOLKS WORKING IN THE FIELDS BEYOND THEM.

YOU COULDN'T HELP BUT NOTICE.

SQUEE

DESPITE EVERYTHING THAT CONFRONTED ME ON THE WAY TO SCHOOL,

I WAS IN HEAVEN ONCE I STEPPED INSIDE IT.

I LOVED GOING TO THE LIBRARY. IT WAS THE FIRST TIME I EVER SAW BLACK NEWSPAPERS AND MAGAZINES LIKE JET, EBONY, THE BALTIMORE AFRO-AMERICAN, OR THE CHICAGO DEFENDER.

AND I'LL NEVER FORGET MY LIBRARIAN, COREEN HARVEY.

MY DEAR CHILDREN, READ. READ EVERYTHING.

BUT SOMETIMES GOING TO SCHOOL WAS A LUXURY
MY FAMILY COULDN'T AFFORD. WHEN PLANTING AND
HARVESTING SEASONS ARRIVED, THE REALITY OF THOSE
FIELDS DISPLACED ANY DREAMS ABOUT THE FUTURE.

I'D PLEAD WITH THEM
TO LET ME GO.

I'D EXPLAIN HOW FAR
BEHIND I'D FALL IF I MISSED
THOSE DAYS OF CLASSWORK.

we need
you here,
Bob.

AND SO I'D HIDE.

AS THE OTHERS MADE THEIR WAY TO THE FIELDS AND THE DAY'S WORK, I WOULD SLIP AWAY.

I WOULD GET UP AND EAT BREAKFAST, LIKE NORMAL.

BOB! where are you?

RRRMMM

MRRMM

RRRMM

THEN,

WHEN I COULD HEAR THE APPROACHING BUS,

I'D DASH OUT

CLIMB ON

AND BE OFF.

WHEN I GOT HOME, MY FATHER WOULD BE FURIOUS.

I WAS CERTAIN HE'D TAN MY HIDE.

NEVER DO IT AGAIN.

BUT HE NEVER DID WHIP ME-- NOT OVER THAT.

I DID IT AGAIN, AND OF COURSE HE WOULD SCOLD ME AGAIN.

BUT DEEP INSIDE I THINK HE KNEW THERE WAS NO STOPPING ME.

THIS WAS A LIFE DECISION I HAD MADE, AND IT WAS NEAR-IMPOSSIBLE TO TURN ME AWAY FROM IT.

ONE MAY MORNING IN 1954, NEAR THE END OF MY FRESHMAN YEAR OF HIGH SCHOOL, I READ A HEADLINE THAT JUST TURNED MY WORLD UPSIDE-DOWN.

THE U.S. SUPREME COURT HAD HANDED DOWN ITS DECISION IN THE SCHOOL DESEGREGATION CASE OF BROWN VS. THE BOARD OF EDUCATION OF TOPEKA.

THE DOCTRINE OF "SEPARATE BUT EQUAL" — UPON WHICH THE ENTIRE INSTITUTION OF SEGREGATION WAS BASED — HAD BEEN RULED **UNCONSTITUTIONAL**.

Montgomery Advertiser

SEGREGATION IN SCHOOLS OUTLAWED!

I WAS SO EXCITED-- SURELY **EVERYTHING** WAS GOING TO CHANGE.

I THOUGHT THAT, COME FALL, I'D BE RIDING A STATE-OF-THE-ART BUS TO A STATE-OF-THE-ART SCHOOL.

AN INTEGRATED SCHOOL.

NOT EVERYBODY WAS SO EXCITED.

don't get in trouble.

don't you get in the way.

BUT MY PARENTS' ATTITUDE DIDN'T BOTHER ME NEARLY AS MUCH AS THOSE AMONG THE MINISTERS AT THE CHURCH, WHO NEVER MENTIONED THESE INJUSTICES IN THEIR SERMONS.

IT DID **NOT** ESCAPE MY NOTICE THAT OUR MINISTER ALWAYS DEPARTED CHURCH IN A **VERY** NICE AUTOMOBILE.

THEN, ONE SUNDAY MORNING IN EARLY 1955, I WAS LISTENING TO **WRMA** OUT OF MONTGOMERY WHEN I HEARD A SERMON BY SOMEONE UNKNOWN TO ME--

A YOUNG PREACHER FROM ATLANTA. I DIDN'T CATCH HIS NAME UNTIL THE VERY END.

CRACKLE
WHRRRR

and so thank you, and again, you just heard DR. MARTIN LUTHER KING, JR. coming up next we've got a real treat for you on this Sunday

DR. KING'S MESSAGE HIT ME LIKE A BOLT OF LIGHTNING. HE APPLIED THE PRINCIPLES OF THE CHURCH TO WHAT WAS HAPPENING NOW, TODAY. IT WAS CALLED THE SOCIAL GOSPEL--

-- AND I FELT LIKE HE WAS PREACHING DIRECTLY TO ME.

I WENT TO THE SCHOOL LIBRARY ON MONDAY TO FIND OUT EVERYTHING I COULD ABOUT THIS MAN.

AT THE TIME, I COULD ONLY FIND ONE NEWSPAPER ARTICLE. BUT 1955 WAS A WATERSHED YEAR.

...to be th...
...t Dr. Martin Lu...
King, Jr., a graduate
of Morehouse College in
Atlanta, GA was appointed
resident pastor of Dexter
Avenue Baptist Church.

...ARBON HILL -81-year
...edell Rodgers is
...to the firs...
...ion of a...

IN MAY, A SECOND SUPREME COURT RULING IN BROWN V. BOARD PROMPTED SEGREGATIONIST ELECTED OFFICIALS, LIKE SENATORS JAMES EASTLAND OF MISSISSIPPI AND STROM THURMOND OF SOUTH CAROLINA, TO SWEAR TO THE DEATH THEIR CONTINUED DEFIANCE OF THE COURT.

LINES HAD BEEN DRAWN. BLOOD WAS BEGINNING TO SPILL.

THAT AUGUST, AN INCIDENT OCCURRED
WHICH **NO ONE** COULD IGNORE.

IN MONEY, MISSISSIPPI, THE BODY OF
FOURTEEN-YEAR OLD **EMMETT TILL**,
WHO WAS DOWN FROM CHICAGO
VISITING RELATIVES, WAS PULLED
FROM THE BOTTOM OF THE
TALLAHATCHIE RIVER.

THE DAY BEFORE, AS HE LEFT
THE MONEY COUNTRY STORE WITH
SOME FRIENDS, EMMETT SAID
"BYE, BABY" TO THE WHITE WOMAN
BEHIND THE COUNTER.

THE NEXT DAY,
HE WAS DEAD.

A BLACK FARMER NAMED MOSES WRIGHT
WITNESSED THE TWO WHITE MEN DRAGGING
EMMETT TILL FROM HIS RELATIVES' HOME,
AND HAD THE COURAGE TO TESTIFY
AGAINST THEM IN OPEN COURT.

THE ALL-WHITE JURY FOUND THOSE TWO
WHITE DEFENDANTS **NOT GUILTY.**

A FEW MONTHS LATER, THEY EVEN CONFESSED
TO THE MURDER IN **LOOK** MAGAZINE, BUT THERE
WAS NOTHING TO BE DONE — THEY HAD ALREADY BEEN TRIED.

THEN, ON DECEMBER 1, 1955, ROSA PARKS REFUSED TO MOVE TO THE BACK OF THE BUS.

IF YOU DON'T MOVE, I'LL BE FORCED TO CALL THE POLICE, AND THEY WILL ARREST YOU.

YOU MAY DO JUST THAT.

MY FAMILY DIDN'T KNOW ROSA PARKS, BUT THEY KNEW PLENTY OF WOMEN LIKE HER. MORE THAN A FEW WIVES AND MOTHERS FROM PIKE COUNTY DID DOMESTIC WORK IN MONTGOMERY.

SHE WAS ARRESTED.

MONTGOMERY WAS JUST FIFTY MILES DOWN THE ROAD FROM US. OUR MINISTER LIVED THERE. MOST OF MY TEACHERS WERE FROM THERE. SO WHEN DR. KING, AS PRESIDENT OF THE MONTGOMERY IMPROVEMENT ASSOCIATION, LED A BOYCOTT OF THOSE BUSES,

WE FELT LIKE WE WERE A PART OF IT, TOO.

58

I LISTENED FIRSTHAND TO ACCOUNTS OF WHAT WAS HAPPENING.

So that's what I did about that, but

Mae, they're empty! every day they'd be full, but there's hardly a soul riding those buses now.

I FOLLOWED IT ALMOST EVERY DAY, EITHER IN THE PAPERS...

50,000 NEGROES ARE BELIEVED TO BE PARTICIPATING AT THIS TIME...

OR ON THE RADIO.

THE BOYCOTT WENT ON FOR MORE THAN A YEAR.

CLIP CLOP

CLIP CLIP CLOP

DR. KING'S EXAMPLE SHOWED ME THAT IT WAS POSSIBLE TO DO MORE AS A MINISTER THAN WHAT I HAD WITNESSED IN MY OWN CHURCH.

I WAS INSPIRED.

SO, FIVE DAYS BEFORE MY SIXTEENTH BIRTHDAY, I PREACHED MY FIRST PUBLIC SERMON--

"A PRAYING MOTHER", FROM THE FIRST BOOK OF SAMUEL.

I WAS NERVOUS,

BUT ONCE I WARMED UP

THE CONGREGATION WARMED UP TOO,

AND OUT POURED THE EMOTIONS.

amen!

praise the Lord!

PFASH! KLIK PFASH!!

AFTER HEARING OF MY SERMON, THE MONTGOMERY ADVERTISER ASKED TO TAKE MY PICTURE FOR AN ARTICLE.

KLIK PFASH!!

THAT WAS THE FIRST TIME I EVER SAW MY NAME IN PRINT.

25¢

MAN FOUND AFTER THREE DAY SEARCH

BOY PREACHER.

WHAT DID YOU DO AFTER HIGH SCHOOL? HOW DID YOU GO TO COLLEGE?

is that where you met Dr. King?

ha! well, YES and NO.

MY MOTHER HELPED ME GO TO COLLEGE...

MY MOTHER HAD A PART-TIME JOB WORKING AT THE WHITE BAPTIST OFFERING HOME IN DOWNTOWN TROY, ALABAMA.

ONE DAY AT WORK, SHE SAW A LITTLE PAPER PUBLISHED BY THE ALABAMA BAPTIST CONVENTION (which was all-white).

IT MENTIONED A SCHOOL IN NASHVILLE CALLED AMERICAN BAPTIST THEOLOGICAL SEMINARY THAT WAS JOINTLY SUPPORTED BY THE WHITE SOUTHERN BAPTISTS AND BLACK NATIONAL BAPTISTS.

AMERICAN BAPTIST SEMIN

ACCORDING TO THE ARTICLE, IT WAS A SCHOOL FOR BLACK MEN AND WOMEN TO STUDY TO BECOME MINISTERS OR MISSIONARIES-- AND IT OFFERED A WORK-STUDY PROGRAM ON CAMPUS.

APPLY HERE.

SO I APPLIED TO
GO TO SCHOOL THERE,

AND WAS ACCEPTED,

AND I GOT A JOB WASHING DISHES
AND SERVING FOOD ON THE LINE.

IT WASN'T GLAMOROUS,

BUT I GOT TO KNOW ALL THE
FACULTY, STUDENTS, AND VISITORS.
EVERYBODY NEEDS TO EAT.

I LOVED THE NEW IDEAS COLLEGE
WAS INTRODUCING ME TO, IN
RELIGION AND PHILOSOPHY--
BUT I COULDN'T STOP THINKING
ABOUT THE SOCIAL GOSPEL.

HERE I WAS READING ABOUT
JUSTICE, WHEN THERE WERE
BRAVE PEOPLE OUT THERE
WORKING TO MAKE IT HAPPEN.

I STARTED TO FEEL GUILTY
FOR NOT DOING MORE.
I BECAME RESTLESS.

I THOUGHT ABOUT **TROY STATE**, JUST A FEW MILES FROM MY PARENTS' HOME, WHERE NO BLACK STUDENT WAS ALLOWED.

SO I APPLIED AS A TRANSFER STUDENT.

ONE MONTH PASSED, THEN ANOTHER. I NEVER HEARD BACK.

FINALLY, I DECIDED TO INTRODUCE MYSELF TO THE ONLY PERSON WHO I THOUGHT COULD UNDERSTAND WHAT I WAS TRYING TO DO:

OVER THE NEXT SEVERAL WEEKS I EXCHANGED A SERIES OF LETTERS AND PHONE CALLS WITH REV. RALPH ABERNATHY AND A LAWYER NAMED FRED GRAY.

EVERYONE KNEW FRED GRAY. HE REPRESENTED ROSA PARKS, AND WAS NOW DR. KING'S ATTORNEY.

FINALLY, GRAY AND ABERNATHY WROTE TO TELL ME THAT DR. KING WANTED TO MEET ME.

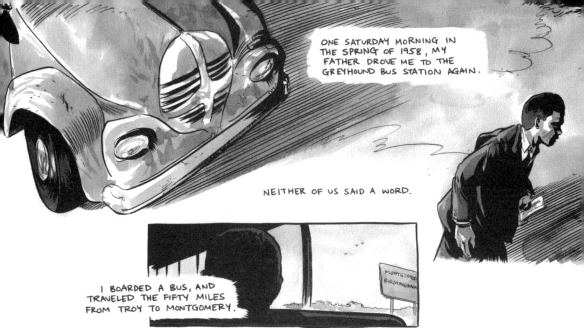

ONE SATURDAY MORNING IN THE SPRING OF 1958, MY FATHER DROVE ME TO THE GREYHOUND BUS STATION AGAIN.

NEITHER OF US SAID A WORD.

I BOARDED A BUS, AND TRAVELED THE FIFTY MILES FROM TROY TO MONTGOMERY.

I'D NEVER SEEN A LAWYER BEFORE-- BLACK OR WHITE.

NOK NOK

ahem

AND I PRESUME YOU'RE JOHN LEWIS?

YES SIR. ATTORNEY GRAY?

WE'RE GOING TO HAVE TO DRIVE OVER TO THE CHURCH.

KLIK KLIK

NOK NOK

come in!

SO--

ARE YOU THE BOY FROM TROY?

ARE YOU JOHN LEWIS?

I JUST WANT TO MEET THE BOY FROM TROY.

I WAS SO SCARED.

WHO IS THIS YOUNG MAN WHO WANTS TO DESEGREGATE TROY STATE?

I DIDN'T KNOW WHAT TO SAY OR DO.

DR. KING, I AM JOHN ROBERT LEWIS.

I SAID MY WHOLE NAME.

DO YOU REALLY WANT TO GO TO TROY STATE?

YES, DR. KING.

I WANT TO GO TO TROY STATE.

THEY QUESTIONED ME ABOUT EVERYTHING--

WELL, YOU KNOW--

WHERE I WAS FROM,

HOW I WAS RAISED,

IF I KNEW WHAT I WOULD REALLY FACE.

MY FATHER DIDN'T SAY A WORD TO ME ON THE RIDE BACK FROM THE BUS STATION, EITHER.

BUT THE NEXT MORNING THEY SAT ME DOWN FOR QUESTIONING, ASKING ME WHAT HAD HAPPENED THE PREVIOUS DAY.

I TOLD THEM.

AT FIRST THEY WANTED TO BE SUPPORTIVE. BUT THEY WERE AFRAID. NOT JUST FOR THEMSELVES, BUT FOR THOSE AROUND US, OUR FRIENDS AND NEIGHBORS.

THEY SAID THEY DIDN'T WANT ANYTHING TO DO WITH FILING A SUIT AGAINST THE STATE OF ALABAMA. NOTHING. NOT ONE THING.

I WAS HEARTBROKEN, BUT IT WAS THEIR DECISION.

I WROTE DR. KING A LETTER EXPLAINING THAT I WOULD BE RETURNING TO **NASHVILLE** IN THE FALL.

LOOKING BACK, IT MUST'VE BEEN THE **SPIRIT OF HISTORY** TAKING HOLD OF MY LIFE--

BECAUSE IN NASHVILLE I'D MEET PEOPLE WHO OPENED MY EYES TO A SENSE OF VALUES THAT WOULD FOREVER DOMINATE MY MORAL PHILOSOPHY--

LEWIS

THE WAY OF PEACE,

THE WAY OF LOVE,

THE WAY OF NON-VIOLENCE.

= KNOCK KNOCK =

COME IN?

ROSA, THANK YOU FOR WAITING. HOW ARE YOU?

I'M GOOD, BOB. ARE YOU READY?

I'M READY.

CONGRESSMAN, BEFORE YOU GO, THERE'S A MESSAGE HERE.

IT'S FROM JIM LAWSON.

MARCH 26, 1958.

I WAS ATTENDING FIRST BAPTIST CHURCH IN DOWNTOWN NASHVILLE.

YOU COULD LITERALLY STAND ON THE STEPS, THROW A BASEBALL, AND HIT THE STEPS OF THE TENNESSEE STATE CAPITOL.

A YOUNG MAN WILL BE JOINING US THIS EVENING, IF YOU'RE INTERESTED.

HE'LL BE CONDUCTING A WORKSHOP ON NON-VIOLENCE HERE AT FIRST BAPTIST--

HIS NAME IS JIM LAWSON.

THE CONGREGATION, LED BY KELLY MILLER SMITH, WERE BLACK BAPTISTS WHO'D LEFT THE WHITE CHURCH BECAUSE THEY HAD BEEN FORCED TO WORSHIP IN THE BALCONY.

I WAS ONE OF THE FIRST VOLUNTEERS TO ATTEND.

YES?

IT WASN'T A VERY LARGE MEETING. I WAS THE ONLY STUDENT TO GO FROM MY LITTLE SCHOOL.

THERE WERE YOUNG PEOPLE LIKE DIANE NASH FROM FISK UNIVERSITY. OTHERS CAME FROM MEHARRY MEDICAL COLLEGE AND TENNESSEE STATE.

AT THE TIME, JIM LAWSON WAS A GRADUATE STUDENT IN THE DIVINITY SCHOOL AT VANDERBILT.

HE ALSO REPRESENTED AN ORGANIZATION CALLED THE FELLOWSHIP OF RECONCILIATION, BETTER KNOWN AS F.O.R., A PACIFIST GROUP COMMITTED TO THE PHILOSOPHY AND DISCIPLINE OF NON-VIOLENCE.

F.O.R. HAD ALSO PUBLISHED A POPULAR COMIC BOOK CALLED MARTIN LUTHER KING AND THE MONTGOMERY STORY, WHICH EXPLAINED THE BASICS OF PASSIVE RESISTANCE AND NON-VIOLENT ACTION AS TOOLS FOR DESEGREGATION.

I WANT TO START WORKING WITH YOUNG PEOPLE, WITH STUDENTS-- HIGH SCHOOL AND COLLEGE STUDENTS.

JIM TALKED ABOUT THE MONTGOMERY BUS BOYCOTT,
ABOUT WAR RESISTANCE,
ABOUT NONVIOLENCE.

HE SPOKE OF **GANDHI**, THIS LITTLE BROWN MAN FROM INDIA USING THE WAY OF NONVIOLENCE TO FREE AN ENTIRE NATION OF PEOPLE.

AND HOW WE COULD APPLY NONVIOLENCE, JUST AS DR. KING DID IN MONTGOMERY, ALL ACROSS AMERICA-- SOUTH **AND** NORTH-- TO ERADICATE SOME OF THE EVILS WE ALL FACED:

THE EVIL OF **RACISM**,

THE EVIL OF **POVERTY**,

THE EVIL OF **WAR**.

JIM LAWSON CONVEYED THE URGENCY OF DEVELOPING OUR PHILOSOPHY, OUR DISCIPLINE, OUR UNDERSTANDING.

HIS WORDS LIBERATED ME.

I THOUGHT, THIS IS IT...

THIS IS THE WAY OUT.

I TOLD MY CLASSMATES.

I TOLD TWO OF MY CLOSEST FRIENDS, BERNARD LAFAYETTE AND JAMES BEVEL.

I TOLD EVERYONE THAT THEY SHOULD COME TO THIS WORKSHOP.

NOK NOK

23

A FEW DAYS LATER WE HAD ANOTHER NON-VIOLENCE WORKSHOP, THIS TIME WITH MINISTERS AND STUDENTS FROM A NUMBER OF DIFFERENT SCHOOLS NEARBY.

BERNARD LAFAYETTE WAS ONE OF THE FIRST PEOPLE TO ATTEND WITH ME.

WE CALLED EACH OTHER NAMES,

YOU SON OF A BITCH!

OVER AND OVER AGAIN.

NIGGER LOVER!

nigger.

IN TIME, EVERYONE PLAYS THE ROLES OF PROTESTERS, THE INSTIGATORS, AND THE RESISTANCE.

THERE MAY BE A BLACK PERSON PLAYING THE ROLE OF A WHITE PERSON, OR VICE VERSA.

WE EACH TRIED TO DO EVERYTHING WE COULD TO TEST OURSELVES, TO BREAK EACH OTHER'S SPIRITS.

WE TRIED TO DEHUMANIZE EACH OTHER.

SOMETIMES I COULDN'T HELP BUT SMILE--
EVEN **LAUGH** -- WHEN SOMEONE PLAYED SUCH
AN UNNATURAL ROLE.

BUT SOMETIMES IT WAS ONE OF YOUR
FRIENDS CALLING YOU NAMES, KNOCKING
YOU DOWN, SPITTING ON YOU.

you okay, charles?

i don't think i can do it.

i just can't.

maybe i can bring signs, or **make** them. maybe i can drive people to the site.

but i can't take it. i **CAN'T** be nonviolent.

I CANNOT.

FOR SOME, IT WAS TOO MUCH.

BUT WE NEEDED TO SEE HOW EACH OF US
WOULD REACT UNDER **STRESS.**

LAWSON TAUGHT US HOW TO PROTECT OURSELVES,

HOW TO **DISARM** OUR ATTACKERS BY CONNECTING WITH THEIR **HUMANITY,**

MAINTAIN EYE CONTACT, JOHN!

HOW TO PROTECT EACH OTHER,

HOW TO **SURVIVE.**

BUT THE HARDEST PART TO LEARN-- TO TRULY **UNDERSTAND,** DEEP IN YOUR HEART--

WAS HOW TO FIND **LOVE** FOR YOUR ATTACKER.

DO **NOT** LET THEM SHAKE YOUR FAITH IN NONVIOLENCE-- <u>LOVE</u> THEM!

WE TOOK A NAME-- **THE NASHVILLE STUDENT MOVEMENT.** BECAUSE OF OUR DISTRUST OF CENTRALIZED POWER, WE INSISTED ON A ROTATING LEADERSHIP.

WE WERE ALL IN THIS **TOGETHER.**

AND WE WERE READY TO **ACT.**

SEGREGATION AT THE DOWNTOWN STORES BOTHERED US THE MOST.

WE COULD SHOP THERE AND PAY THE SAME PRICES AS WHITE CUSTOMERS, BUT WE COULDN'T USE THE DRESSING ROOMS, OR SIT AT THE LUNCH COUNTER TO EAT.

IT WAS HUMILIATING.

SO WE DECIDED THE DEPARTMENT STORE LUNCH COUNTERS WOULD BE OUR FIRST TARGET.

NOVEMBER 28, 1959.

WE STARTED WITH "TEST SIT-INS" TO TEST THE LOCAL STORES' POLICIES, ESTABLISHING THAT THEY WOULD **NOT** SERVE AN INTERRACIAL OR ALL-BLACK GROUP.

OUR PLAN WAS SIMPLE. ENTER A STORE, ASK TO BE SERVED, AND IF--OR **WHEN**-- WE WERE REFUSED, WE WOULD LEAVE.

I WAS NERVOUS.

WE WERE **ALL** NERVOUS.

CH-CHING!

WE EACH PURCHASED SOMETHING, ESTABLISHING US AS LEGITIMATE PAYING CUSTOMERS, AND THEN SAT DOWN AT THE LUNCH COUNTER FOR A BITE TO EAT.

CLIP

CLIP

CLIP

CLIP

UM,

I'M SORRY, WE CAN'T SERVE YOU HERE.

MAY WE SPEAK TO THE MANAGER?

PART OF OUR DISCIPLINE WAS THAT ONLY ONE PERSON SPOKE FOR THE GROUP IN AN ACTION. ON THIS DAY, WE DESIGNATED DIANE.

KLAK

KLIK

KLAK

KLAK

No harsh words.
No violence.

No one even paid much attention as we left.

When news of this student-led campaign spread, words of encouragement and support flowed in from around the country.

We decided to stage our second test sit-in the following Saturday, December 5th.

HOLD UP.

WE DON'T **SERVE** COLORED PEOPLE HERE.

THIS TIME, I THINK THEY WERE **EXPECTING** US.

MAY I SPEAK TO THE MANAGER, PLEASE?

I'M SORRY, IT'S STORE POLICY NOT TO SERVE NEGROES.

THANK YOU.

AND SO AGAIN, WE LEFT WITHOUT INCIDENT.

IN JANUARY, FOLLOWING THE WINTER BREAK FROM SCHOOL, OUR WEEKLY WORKSHOP NUMBERS SWELLED.

WE WERE CLOSE TO READY, THOUGH NO SPECIFIC DATE HAD YET BEEN SET FOR OUR FIRST SIT-IN. AS FATE-- OR THE SPIRIT OF HISTORY-- WOULD HAVE IT, SOMEONE ELSE MADE THE MOVE **FOR** US.

ON MONDAY, FEBRUARY 1, 1960 IN GREENSBORO, NORTH CAROLINA, FOUR FRESHMEN FROM NORTH CAROLINA A+T TOOK SEATS AT THE DOWNTOWN WOOLWORTH'S LUNCH COUNTER.

ONE OF THEM HAD READ THE **F.O.R.** COMIC ABOUT DR. KING AND MONTGOMERY, WHICH GOT THEM TALKING ABOUT NONVIOLENT ACTION.

I'M SORRY, BUT IT'S AGAINST STORE POLICY TO SERVE COLORED PEOPLE

THE NEXT DAY, NINETEEN STUDENTS -- BLACK **AND** WHITE -- HAD JOINED THE ORIGINAL FOUR AT WOOLWORTH'S.

BY WEDNESDAY, THE NUMBER SWELLED TO **85**, AND SIMILAR SIT-INS HAD FORMED IN **RALEIGH** AND DURHAM.

F.W. WOOLWORTH'S

A YOUNG NORTH CAROLINA MINISTER, **DOUGLAS MOORE**, WAS A FRIEND OF JIM LAWSON AND CALLED TO ENCOURAGE US.

they've been preparing... mm-hm.

that's right. we've had TWO. they're nearly ready.

DING!

ON FEBRUARY 7ᵀᴴ, ONE WEEK AFTER THE GREENSBORO SIT-INS, WE BEGAN OURS.

I'M GOING TO BE INSIDE. I WON'T NEED IT, SIR.

SERIOUSLY, TAKE IT.

thank you, brother.

OKAY, I'M GOING TO WEAR THE SCARF--AND I APPRECIATE IT-- BUT YOU ALL REALLY DON'T HAVE TO GO TO ALL THIS TROUBLE.

THERE WAS A HALF FOOT OF SNOW ON THE GROUND IN NASHVILLE THE DAY WE FIRST SAT-IN, AND I SURVIVED THAT...

11:00 AM, FEBRUARY 7th, 1960.

90

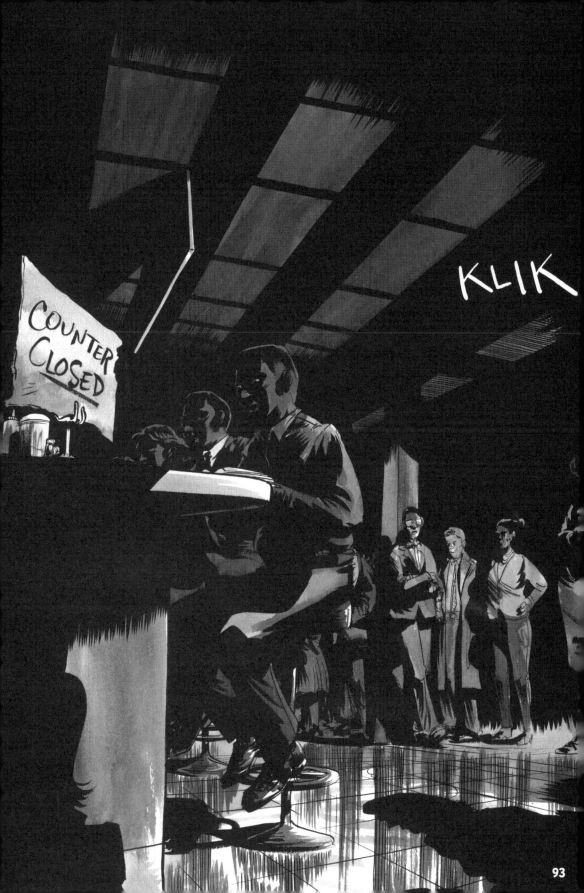

IS EVERYONE OKAY?

WE SAT IN THAT EERIE QUIET FOR SEVERAL HOURS.

COUNTER CLOSED

FINE, JOHN. A LITTLE HARD TO READ IN THE DARK, BUT WE'RE GETTING ENOUGH THROUGH THE WINDOWS TO MAKE DO.

EVENTUALLY, THE CALM WAS BROKEN.

what the hell is this?!

niggers! go home.

what are y'all even doing here?!

get outta here, niggers--y'all don't belong!

BUT AFTER A WHILE, THEY WORE THEMSELVES OUT AND LEFT.

AT ABOUT SIX THAT EVENING, WORD CAME THAT IT WAS TIME TO GO.

WHEN WE GOT BACK TO FIRST BAPTIST CHURCH, IT WAS LIKE NEW YEAR'S EVE.

THE OTHER TEAMS AT KRESS'S AND McCLELLAN'S HAD BEEN JUST AS SUCCESSFUL.

THAT WAITRESS WAS SO SCARED, SO NERVOUS, SHE DIDN'T KNOW WHAT TO DO! HER HANDS WERE SHAKING AND SHE STARTED DROPPING DISHES RIGHT ON THE FLOOR!

YOU WOULDN'T BELIEVE IT, DIANE!

WHEN WE WENT TO USE THE LADIES' ROOM...

LADIES
WHITE ONLY

LADIES
WHITE ONLY

LADIES
WHITE ONLY

OH!

NIGRAS, NIGRAS EVERYWHERE!

OUR NUMBERS SWELLED TO OVER **200** STUDENTS FOR OUR NEXT SIT-IN ON THURSDAY, FEBRUARY 18th.

AGAIN, THE COUNTER WAS CLOSED.

W.T. GRANT

THAT AFTERNOON, WE STAYED FOR HOURS WITHOUT INCIDENT

W.T. GRANT

TWO DAYS LATER, WE MARCHED AGAIN.

here come the niggers again.

PEOPLE WERE STARTING TO **NOTICE.**

where am **I** supposed to eat lunch?

go home, nigger--you're not welcome!

GO BACK TO _AFRICA!_

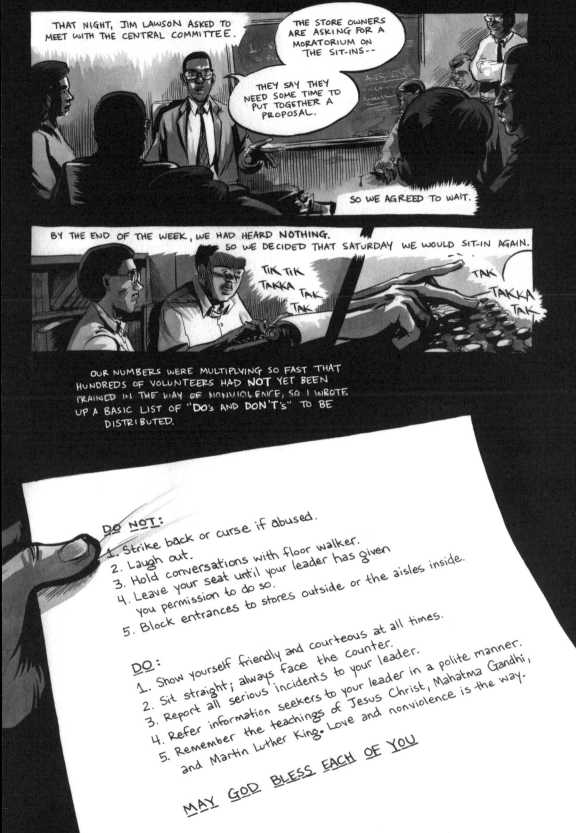

ON THE MORNING OF FEBRUARY 27th, 1960, WE GATHERED TO HEAR **WILL CAMPBELL**, A WHITE MINISTER WHO'D BEEN RUN OUT OF OXFORD, MISSISSIPPI, FOR PLAYING **PING-PONG** WITH A BLACK MAN.

THE DAY BEFORE, WE'D GOTTEN WORD FROM NASHVILLE'S CHIEF OF POLICE THAT ANYONE INVOLVED IN FURTHER PROTESTS WOULD BE ARRESTED.

THERE WERE ALSO RUMORS OF PLANNED ATTACKS BY YOUNG WHITES, WHICH THE POLICE DID **NOT** INTEND TO STOP.

SO ON THIS PARTICULAR MORNING, WILL CAMPBELL HAD COME TO TELL US WHAT HE HAD HEARD FROM HIS CONTACTS IN THE WHITE COMMUNITY.

IF YOU ATTEMPT TO SIT-IN, THE BUSINESS COMMUNITY, THE LOCAL OFFICIALS, AND THE AUTHORITIES WILL ALL PULL BACK--

THEY WILL **LET** POLICE AND... THE **ROUGH** ELEMENT IN THE WHITE COMMUNITY COME INTO THE STORES AND **BEAT** YOU.

BUT IT IS **YOUR** DECISION.

WE KNEW WE COULDN'T LET THE THREAT OF VIOLENCE STOP US.

WE WERE **GOING** TO SIT-IN.

MY GROUP TARGETED WOOLWORTH'S.

NO SOONER DID WE TAKE OUR SEATS AT THE UPSTAIRS COUNTER THAN SOME YOUNG MEN BEGAN ATTACKING THE GROUP DOWNSTAIRS.

WE IMMEDIATELY WENT DOWN TO JOIN OUR BROTHERS AND SISTERS.

VIOLENCE DOES
BEGET VIOLENCE,

BUT THE OPPOSITE IS JUST AS TRUE.

FURY SPENDS ITSELF PRETTY QUICKLY WHEN THERE'S NO FURY FACING IT.

THE BEATING SUBSIDED.

THE GROUP AT **KRESS'S** FACED HUMILIATION.

CHATTANOOGA

AT McCLELLAN'S, PAUL LAPRAD DREW PARTICULAR ATTENTION FOR BEING WHITE.

THE POLICE, CONSPICUOUSLY **ABSENT** WHILE WE WERE BEATEN, ARRIVED QUICKLY AFTER THE MOB WORE THEMSELVES OUT.

IF YOU DO NOT MOVE FROM YOUR SEATS AND <u>LEAVE</u> THIS ESTABLISHMENT, YOU <u>WILL</u> BE PLACED UNDER ARREST!

WE DIDN'T.

WE WANTED TO **CHANGE** AMERICA -- TO MAKE IT SOMETHING DIFFERENT, SOMETHING **BETTER.**

whites this way, colored to THAT wagon--

cmon now!

WE SHALL OVERCOME ♪

WE SHALL OVER COME ♪

THERE WERE SO MANY OF US TO ARREST THAT AS THEY DROVE US OFF TO JAIL,

WE FILLED EVERY PADDY WAGON THE POLICE HAD IN NASHVILLE.

WE SHALL ♪ OVERCOME ♪ SOMEDAY ♪♪

Woolworth's

FEBRUARY 27, 1960 WAS MY FIRST ARREST,

THE FIRST OF MANY.

WE WERE JUBILANT AS WE FILLED THE JAIL CELLS.

we shall all be free

we shall all be free

we shall all be free someday

SURROUNDED BY SO MANY OF OUR FRIENDS, WE FELT LIKE PRISONERS IN A HOLY WAR.

we are ALL Not ALONE

BACK AT THE LUNCH COUNTERS, POLICE COULD HARDLY KEEP UP WITH THE WAVES OF STUDENTS QUICKLY FILLING THE EMPTY SEATS. NO SOONER WOULD ONE GROUP BE ARRESTED THAN ANOTHER WOULD TAKE ITS PLACE.

we are not ALONE

82 OF US WENT TO JAIL THAT DAY.

we are not ALONE

we are not ALONE someday

THE POLICE WANTED NOTHING MORE THAN TO BE **RID** OF US, SO THEY REDUCED THE BAIL FROM $100 TO $5 APIECE.

BUT IT DIDN'T MATTER.

WE WEREN'T ABOUT TO COOPERATE IN **ANY** WAY WITH THE SYSTEM ALLOWING THE VERY DISCRIMINATION WE WERE PROTESTING.

WE SHALL OVERCO...

WE SHALL OVERCOME

WE SHALL OVERCOME SOMEDAY ♩

♩ WE SHALL ALL BE FR...

IT DIDN'T TAKE NASHVILLE'S POWERS-THAT-BE LONG TO REALIZE IT WAS IMPOSSIBLE TO FORCE US TO PAY OUR WAY OUT.

AROUND 11:00 P.M., WE WERE ALL RELEASED.

CL-CLANK

THAT SUNDAY MORNING, FISK UNIVERSITY PRESIDENT DR. STEPHEN J. WRIGHT ADDRESSED MORE THAN 1,000 STUDENTS JAMMED INTO THE UNIVERSITY CHAPEL.

TO THE STUDENTS WHO TOOK PART IN YESTERDAY'S ACTIONS, I SAY TO YOU-- I STAND WITH YOU.

NASHVILLE STANDS WITH YOU.

DR. WRIGHT WAS THE FIRST BLACK COLLEGE PRESIDENT IN THE COUNTRY TO TAKE SUCH A STAND.

WE WERE EUPHORIC.

THE NEXT DAY WE ALL WENT TO COURT.

THREE AMAZING LAWYERS CAME TO OUR DEFENSE, REFUSING TO CHARGE EVEN A DIME.

Z. ALEXANDER LOOBY, AN OLDER MAN FROM THE WEST INDIES, WAS OUR LEAD ATTORNEY, AND THE FIRST BLACK MAN ON NASHVILLE'S CITY COUNCIL IN FORTY YEARS. HE HAD ALSO WORKED WITH THURGOOD MARSHALL.

FIRST OFF, Y'ALL SHOULD KNOW WE'RE GONNA BE TRYING THE DEFENDANTS IN GROUPS OF HALF A DOZEN OR SO.

YOUR HONOR, I OBJECT--

OVERRULED.

YOUR HONOR--

I MUST MAKE A FORMAL MOTION THAT THE DEFENDANTS BE TRIED INDIVIDUALLY. THEY DO HAVE A RIGHT TO A FAIR TRIAL.

MOTION DENIED.

SO THE TRIAL PROCEEDED.

THESE YOUNG PEOPLE WERE NOT DISTURBING THE PEACE-- FAR FROM IT.

THEY WERE PEACEFUL CUSTOMERS, FULLY COMPLIANT WITH THE LAW, WHO WERE HARASSED AND BEATEN.

SWIVEL

oh, what's the use!

Scribble
scribble

HAVING HEARD ALL THE EVIDENCE PRESENTED BEFORE ME TODAY,

I FIND THE DEFENDANTS **GUILTY** AND ORDER THEM TO PAY A FINE OF $50 EACH, OR SERVE 30 DAYS IN THE COUNTY WORKHOUSE.

SQUEEK

WAIT?

YOUR HONOR--

WE FEEL THAT BY PAYING THESE FINES, WE WOULD BE CONTRIBUTING TO, AND **SUPPORTING**, THE INJUSTICES AND IMMORAL PRACTICES THAT HAVE BEEN PERFORMED IN THE ARREST AND CONVICTION OF THE DEFENDANTS.

thank you.

JAIL, NO BAIL!

JAIL, NO BAIL!

JAIL, NO BAIL!

AIL, O BAIL!

JAI NO B

JAIL, NO BAIL!

BAM

JAIL, NO BAIL!

JAIL, NO BAIL!

JAIL, NO BAIL!

WHEN THE CITY FOLLOWED THROUGH WITH ITS WORKHOUSE ROUTINE, IT PROMPTED OUTRAGE FROM ALL OVER THE COUNTRY. TELEGRAMS OF SUPPORT ARRIVED FROM RALPH BUNCHE, ELEANOR ROOSEVELT, AND HARRY BELAFONTE.

AT THE SAME TIME, **MORE** STUDENTS VOLUNTEERED AND THE SIT-INS CONTINUED.

MUCH LIKE NASHVILLE ITSELF, **MAYOR BEN WEST** HAD A RELATIVELY PROGRESSIVE REPUTATION ON RACE. IT DID **NOT**, HOWEVER, NECESSARILY MEAN HE WAS WILLING TO RISK HIS JOB AND REPUTATION TO HELP.

BUT ON MARCH 3rd, MAYOR WEST ORDERED OUR **RELEASE**.

WE LEFT JAIL WITH A SENSE OF TRIUMPH, AND WEST ALSO FORMED A BIRACIAL COMMITTEE TO STUDY SEGREGATION IN THE CITY. IN RETURN, HE ASKED US TO TEMPORARILY HALT OUR SIT-INS WHILE THE COMMITTEE WORKED, AND WE AGREED.

THAT SAME DAY, THE CHANCELLOR AND TRUSTEES OF VANDERBILT UNIVERSITY ORDERED THE DEAN OF THE DIVINITY SCHOOL TO DISMISS JIM LAWSON.

CUT OFF THE HEAD, THE THINKING WENT, AND THE BODY WOULD FALL.

109

BUT FOR VANDERBILT, THINGS DIDN'T WORK OUT AS PLANNED. INSTEAD, DOZENS OF FACULTY AND STAFF THREATENED TO RESIGN IN PROTEST, MAKING NATIONAL HEADLINES.

BY THE END OF THE MONTH WE DECIDED WE'D WAITED LONG ENOUGH, SO ON FRIDAY THE 25th, MORE THAN A HUNDRED OF US MARCHED FROM FIRST BAPTIST CHURCH TO NINE DOWNTOWN STORES.

THERE WERE NO ARRESTS THAT DAY, BUT AFTER TENNESSEE GOVERNOR BUFORD ELLINGTON SAW FOOTAGE OF THE DAY'S PROTEST ON THE NATIONAL NEWS, HE WAS IRATE.

THESE SIT-INS ARE INSTIGATED BY, AND STAGED FOR THE CONVENIENCE OF, THE COLUMBIA BROADCAST SYSTEM.

DON'T BUY DOWNT

HELP US END SEGREGATION IN NAS

QUIETLY -- ALMOST INVISIBLY -- WITHIN THE LOCAL CHURCHES, A BLACK COMMUNITY BOYCOTT OF ALL DOWNTOWN STORES BEGAN -- WHAT SOME PEOPLE CALLED A "SELECTIVE BUYING CAMPAIGN."

WOULD EVERYONE IN THE CONGREGATION WHO HAS NOT SPENT ANY MONEY DOWNTOWN PLEASE STAND?

HALLELUJAH!

SIR, YOU'RE THE OWNER OF THIS ESTABLISHMENT. CAN YOU TELL US WHAT BUSINESS HAS BEEN LIKE?

You could roll a BOWLING BALL down Church street, and not hit anybody.

ON APRIL 5TH, THOSE EMPTY STREETS BROUGHT AN OFFER FROM THE MAYOR'S COMMITTEE. IT PROPOSED A SYSTEM OF "PARTIAL INTEGRATION"--

WHICH WAS THE SAME TO US AS PARTIAL SEGREGATION.

BUT IT WAS SUPPORTED BY TWO BLACK COMMITTEE MEMBERS--FISK PRESIDENT WRIGHT, AND T.S.U. PRESIDENT W.S. DAVIS. THIS FELT LIKE BETRAYAL, AND WAS MORE EVIDENCE OF THE DIFFERENCES BETWEEN OUR GENERATIONS.

WE SAW THAT EVIDENCE THE NEXT TIME THURGOOD MARSHALL SPOKE AT FISK.

LOOK, ONCE YOU'VE BEEN ARRESTED, YOU'VE MADE YOUR POINT.

IF SOMEONE OFFERS TO GET YOU OUT, MAN-- GET OUT!

THURGOOD MARSHALL WAS A GOOD MAN, BUT LISTENING TO HIM SPEAK CONVINCED ME, MORE THAN EVER, THAT OUR REVOLT WAS AS MUCH AGAINST THE TRADITIONAL BLACK LEADERSHIP STRUCTURE AS IT WAS AGAINST SEGREGATION AND DISCRIMINATION.

FIVE DAYS AFTER MARSHALL SPOKE, WE RESUMED THE SIT-INS.

THE NEXT WEEKEND--EASTER--A CONFERENCE ORGANIZED BY ELLA BAKER OF SCLC* WAS HELD AT SHAW UNIVERSITY IN RALEIGH.

BAKER ASKED JIM LAWSON, WHOSE MESSAGE APPEALED TO THE YOUNG PEOPLE LISTENING, TO GIVE THE KEYNOTE SPEECH.

THE NAACP** IS TOO CONSERVATIVE--

* SOUTHERN CHRISTIAN LEADERSHIP CONFERENCE
** NATIONAL ASSOCIATION FOR THE ADVANCEMENT OF COLORED PEOPLE

WE MUST TAP INTO OUR GREATEST RESOURCE, A PEOPLE NO LONGER THE VICTIMS OF RACIAL EVIL, WHO CAN ACT IN A DISCIPLINED MANNER TO IMPLEMENT THE CONSTITUTION.

THE WEEKEND CLOSED WITH THE CREATION OF A STUDENT-RUN GROUP THAT WOULD COORDINATE AND ORGANIZE THE ENTIRE SIT-IN MOVEMENT,

AND WHATEVER LAY BEYOND.

THAT ORGANIZATION BECAME KNOWN AS THE STUDENT NONVIOLENT COORDINATING COMMITTEE, OR SNCC-- WHICH WE PRONOUNCED SIMPLY AS "SNICK".

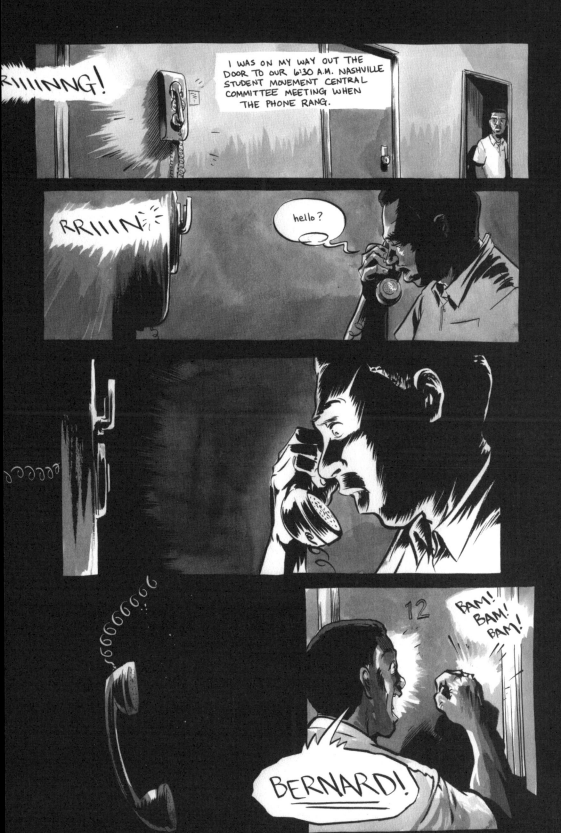

BY NOON, THOUSANDS OF PEOPLE HAD GATHERED AT TENNESSEE STATE TO MARCH ON CITY HALL.

MAYOR WEST--

WE ARE OUTRAGED AT THIS BOMBING! HOW CAN YOU ALLOW THIS SORT OF BEHAVIOR IN NASHVILLE?! IT'S A MIRACLE NO ONE WAS KILLED!

MR. VIVIAN, LET ME SAY--

NO, I'LL SAY.

THIS HAS GONE TOO FAR.

look,

you all have the power to DESTROY this city, so let's not have any mobs. I will do EVERYTHING I can to enforce the laws without prejudice--

but I have NO power to force restaurant owners to serve people they don't want to.

WE ARE ALL CHRISTIANS TOGETHER-- SO LET US PRAY TOGETHER.

HOW ABOUT EATING TOGETHER?!

MAYOR WEST--

WILL YOU USE THE PRESTIGE OF YOUR OFFICE TO APPEAL TO THE CITIZENS TO STOP RACIAL DISCRIMINATION?

I APPEAL TO ALL CITIZENS TO END DISCRIMINATION. TO HAVE NO BIGOTRY,

NO BIAS,

NO HATRED.

end book one.

ACKNOWLEDGMENTS

I am deeply grateful to Andrew Aydin for all of his hard work. He had a vision, and he never gave up. I believe together we have created something truly meaningful. I want to thank Nate Powell for his unbelievable talent, kind spirit, and hard work. He is a wonderful collaborator. And I want to thank Chris Staros, Brett Warnock, Leigh Walton, Chris Ross, and everyone at Top Shelf for their openness, their support, and their powerful work.

John Lewis

I want to thank my Mom for the opportunities in my life that her hard work and sacrifice made possible. I am forever indebted to John Lewis for his remarkable life, his trust, his faith, and his friendship. I am in awe of Nate Powell's talent and grateful to work with him. I want to thank Sara for her patience and support, Vaughn for his guidance and friendship, and Dom for reminding me to have fun. I wish Jordan could see this. And thank you Mr. Parker, Mrs. Fuentes, Jacob Gillison, A.D., Professor Uchimura and all of the teachers and mentors that gave me the courage to walk this road.

Andrew Aydin

I'd like to dedicate my work on this book to the memory of Sarah Kirsch (1970–2012), whose compassion, humanity, vision, and talent deeply shaped the direction of my life from my early teenage years; to my wife Rachel, a true original and cranky do-gooder committed to helping those who need a hand; and to our amazing daughter Harper, in hopes of her growing into a world more humane, more considerate, more loving—a world she and her entire generation will inherit. Let's make the world worth it.

Nate Powell

ABOUT THE AUTHORS

JOHN LEWIS is the U.S. Representative for Georgia's fifth congressional district and an American icon widely known for his role in the civil rights movement.

Photo by Eric Etheridge

As a student at American Baptist Theological Seminary in 1959, Lewis organized sit-in demonstrations at segregated lunch counters in Nashville, Tennessee. In 1961, he volunteered to participate in the Freedom Rides, which challenged segregation at interstate bus terminals across the South. He was beaten severely by angry mobs and arrested by police for challenging the injustice of "Jim Crow" segregation in the South.

From 1963 to 1966, Lewis was Chairman of the Student Nonviolent Coordinating Committee (SNCC). As head of SNCC, Lewis became a nationally recognized figure, dubbed one of the "Big Six" leaders of the civil rights movement. At the age of 23, he was an architect of and a keynote speaker at the historic March on Washington in August 1963.

In 1964, John Lewis coordinated SNCC efforts to organize voter registration drives and community action programs during the Mississippi Freedom Summer. The following year, Lewis helped spearhead one of the most seminal moments of the civil rights movement. Together with Hosea Williams, another notable civil rights leader, John Lewis led over 600 peaceful, orderly protesters across the Edmund Pettus Bridge in Selma, Alabama, on March 7, 1965. They intended to march from Selma to Montgomery to demonstrate the need for voting rights in the state. The marchers were attacked by Alabama state troopers in a brutal confrontation that became known as "Bloody Sunday." News broadcasts and photographs revealing the senseless cruelty of the segregated South helped hasten the passage of the Voting Rights Act of 1965.

Despite physical attacks, serious injuries, and more than 40 arrests, John Lewis remained a devoted advocate of the philosophy of nonviolence. After leaving SNCC in 1966, he continued to work for civil rights, first as Associate Director of the Field Foundation, then with the Southern Regional Council, where he became Executive Director of the Voter Education Project (VEP). In 1977, Lewis was appointed by President Jimmy Carter to direct more than 250,000 volunteers of ACTION, the federal volunteer agency.

In 1981, Lewis was elected to the Atlanta City Council. He was elected to the U.S. House of Representatives in November 1986 and has represented Georgia's fifth district there ever since. In 2011 he was awarded the Medal of Freedom by President Barack Obama.

Lewis's 1998 memoir, *Walking with the Wind: A Memoir of the Movement*, won numerous honors, including the Robert F. Kennedy, Lillian Smith, and Anisfield-Wolf Book Awards. His subsequent book, *Across That Bridge: Life Lessons and a Vision for Change*, won the NAACP Image Award.

(From left to right): Nate Powell, Congressman John Lewis, Andrew Aydin.   Photo by Sandi Villarreal

ANDREW AYDIN, an Atlanta native, currently serves as Digital Director & Policy Advisor in the Washington, D.C., office of Rep. John Lewis. After learning that his boss had been inspired as a young man by the 1950s comic book *Martin Luther King & The Montgomery Story*, Aydin conceived the *March* series and collaborated with Rep. Lewis to write it, while also composing a master's thesis on the history and impact of *The Montgomery Story*. Today, he continues to write comics and lecture about the history of comics in the civil rights movement.

Previously, he served as Communications Director and Press Secretary during Rep. Lewis's 2008 and 2010 re-election campaigns, as District Aide to Rep. John Larson (D-CT), and as Special Assistant to Connecticut Lt. Governor Kevin Sullivan. Aydin is a graduate of the Lovett School in Atlanta, Trinity College in Hartford, and Georgetown University in Washington, D.C. Visit www.andrewaydin.com for more information.

NATE POWELL is a *New York Times* best-selling graphic novelist born in Little Rock, Arkansas, in 1978. He began self-publishing at age 14, and graduated from School of Visual Arts in 2000.

His work includes *You Don't Say, Any Empire, Swallow Me Whole, The Silence of Our Friends, The Year of the Beasts*, and Rick Riordan's *The Lost Hero*. Powell's comics have received such honors as the Eisner Award, two Ignatz Awards, four YALSA Great Graphic Novels for Teens selections, and a *Los Angeles Times* Book Prize finalist selection.

In addition to *March*, Powell has spoken about his work at the United Nations and created animated illustrations for SPLC's documentary *Selma: The Bridge to the Ballot*.

Powell is currently writing and drawing his next book, *Cover*, and drawing *Two Dead* with writer Van Jansen. He lives in Bloomington, Indiana. Visit Nate's website at www.seemybrotherdance.org for more information.

March: Book One © 2013 John Lewis and Andrew Aydin.

Written by John Lewis and Andrew Aydin
Art by Nate Powell

Editor-in-Chief: Chris Staros

Published by Top Shelf Productions, an imprint of IDW Publishing, a division of Idea and Design Works, LLC. Offices: Top Shelf Productions, c/o Idea & Design Works, LLC, 2765 Truxtun Road, San Diego, CA 92106. Top Shelf Productions®, the Top Shelf logo, Idea and Design Works®, and the IDW logo are registered trademarks of Idea and Design Works, LLC. All Rights Reserved. With the exception of small excerpts of artwork used for review purposes, none of the contents of this publication may be reprinted without the permission of IDW Publishing. IDW Publishing does not read or accept unsolicited submissions of ideas, stories, or artwork.

Edited by Chris Staros with Leigh Walton
Designed by Chris Ross and Nate Powell
Cover Coloring on Three-Volume Slipcase Edition: José Villarrubia

Visit our online catalog at www.topshelfcomix.com.

Printed in Korea.

2023   2022   2021   15   16   17   18